DO YOU REALLY WANT TO VISIT URANUS?

BY BRIDGET HEOS

ILLUSTRATED BY DANIELE FABBRI

Amicus Illustrated is published by Amicus
P.O. Box 1329, Mankato, MN 56002
www.amicuspublishing.us

Library of Congress Cataloging-in-Publication Data
Heos, Bridget.
Do you really want to visit Uranus? / by Bridget Heos;
illustrated by Daniele Fabbri. — 1st ed.
p. cm. — (Do you really want to visit–?)
Audience: K-3.
Summary: "A child astronaut takes an imaginary trip
to Uranus, learns about the harsh conditions on the
planet, and decides that Earth is a good home after all.
Includes solar system diagram, Uranus vs. Earth fact
chart, and glossary"–Provided by publisher.
Includes bibliographical references.
ISBN 978-1-60753-202-6 (library binding) —
ISBN 978-1-60753-408-2 (ebook)
1. Uranus (Planet)–Juvenile literature. I. Fabbri, Daniele,
1978– ill. II. Title. III. Series: Do you really want to visit–?
QB681.H46 2013
523.47–dc23   2012026005

Editor: Rebecca Glaser
Designer: The Design Lab

Printed in the United States of America at
Corporate Graphics in North Mankato, Minnesota.

Date 102113   PO 1181

9 8 7 6 5 4 3 2

So you want to go to Uranus. You could be the first person to take pictures of the planet up close. But do you *really* want to go to Uranus?

3

-357 °F

-216 °C

4

Uranus is freezing! Pack a coat! And the world's warmest space suit and spaceship. Make sure the space suit will fit you as a teenager. It could take nine years to get there!

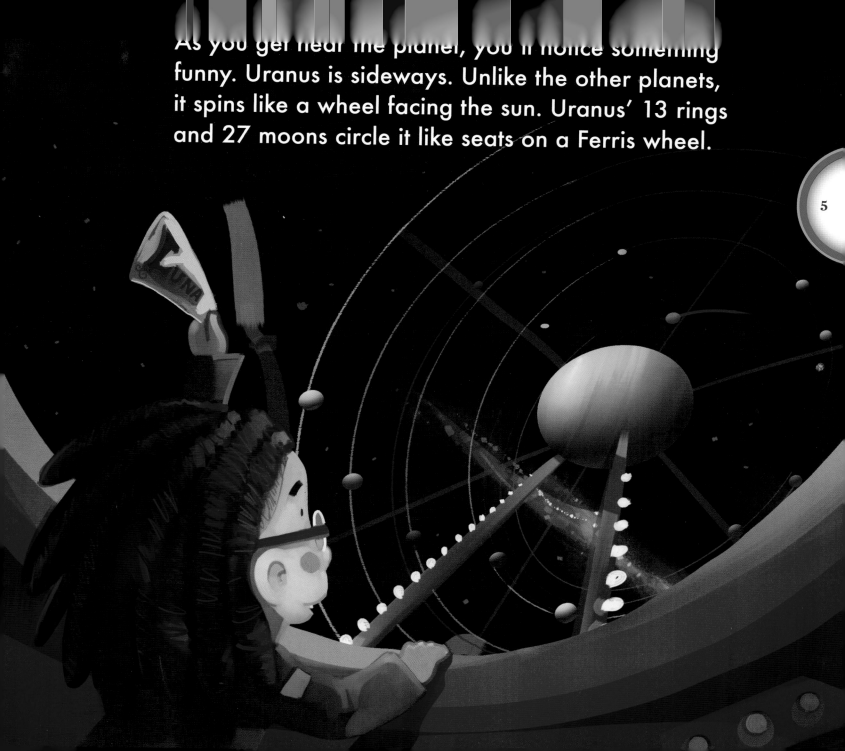

As you get near the planet, you'll notice something funny. Uranus is sideways. Unlike the other planets, it spins like a wheel facing the sun. Uranus' 13 rings and 27 moons circle it like seats on a Ferris wheel.

5

Uranus is also bluer than any earthly blue sky.
It's breathtaking. Literally. Grab your gas mask.
The lovely atmosphere is poisonous to breathe.

You'll reach the clouds of Uranus first. Here, hurricane-force winds blow. Good thing your spaceship is windproof! The wind blows hardest at the poles. Uranus is sideways. You are at a pole when you are closest to the sun.

At least you're on the sunny side of the planet. Good news: it's summer here. Bad news: it's still freezing. Uranus is just so far from the sun! At the opposite pole, winter is cold *and* dark.

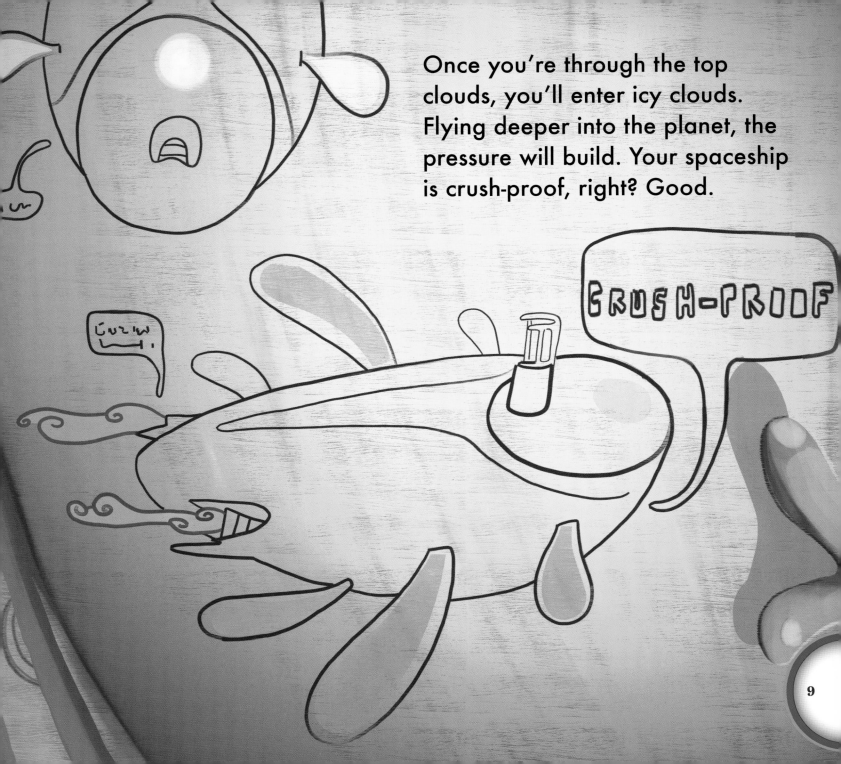

Once you're through the top clouds, you'll enter icy clouds. Flying deeper into the planet, the pressure will build. Your spaceship is crush-proof, right? Good.

You've got a long way to go. Uranus is a gas giant. Most of the planet is made of the gases hydrogen, helium, and methane.

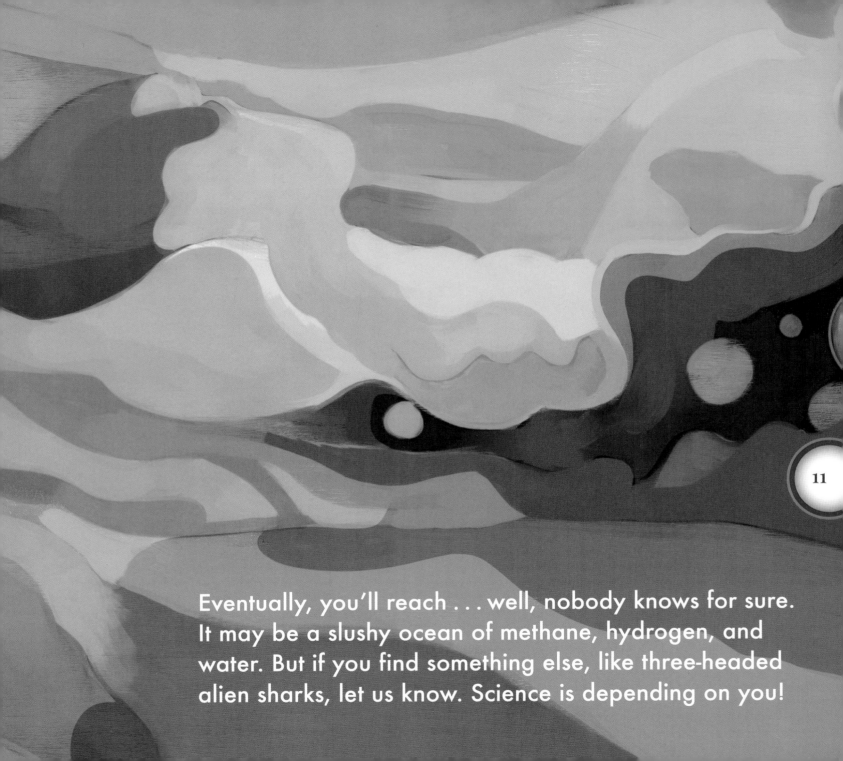

11

Eventually, you'll reach . . . well, nobody knows for sure. It may be a slushy ocean of methane, hydrogen, and water. But if you find something else, like three-headed alien sharks, let us know. Science is depending on you!

If you have a heatproof scuba suit, dive down. Find out whether Uranus has a solid core. Nobody knows that, either.

Remember: making discoveries is great. But safety comes first. On that note, what are you doing here? No human could ever survive on Uranus. Quick! Back in the spaceship.

13

On the way home, you can explore a few of Uranus' 27 moons. Their names are lovely: Cordelia, Ophelia, Juliet... A far cry from "Uranus!"

Cordelia and Ophelia are shepherd moons. They keep one of Uranus' 13 rings in its place.

14

Next, look for Ariel. Many
moons of Uranus are dark.
But Ariel is smooth and bright.

15

Ophelia

Don't miss Umbriel. Shining through the darkness is a bright ring-shaped landform. It's called the "fluorescent Cheerio." Talk about a tourist trap! Oh, look! You're first in line. Find out why the ring is so bright. Is it a crater? Is it covered with frost?

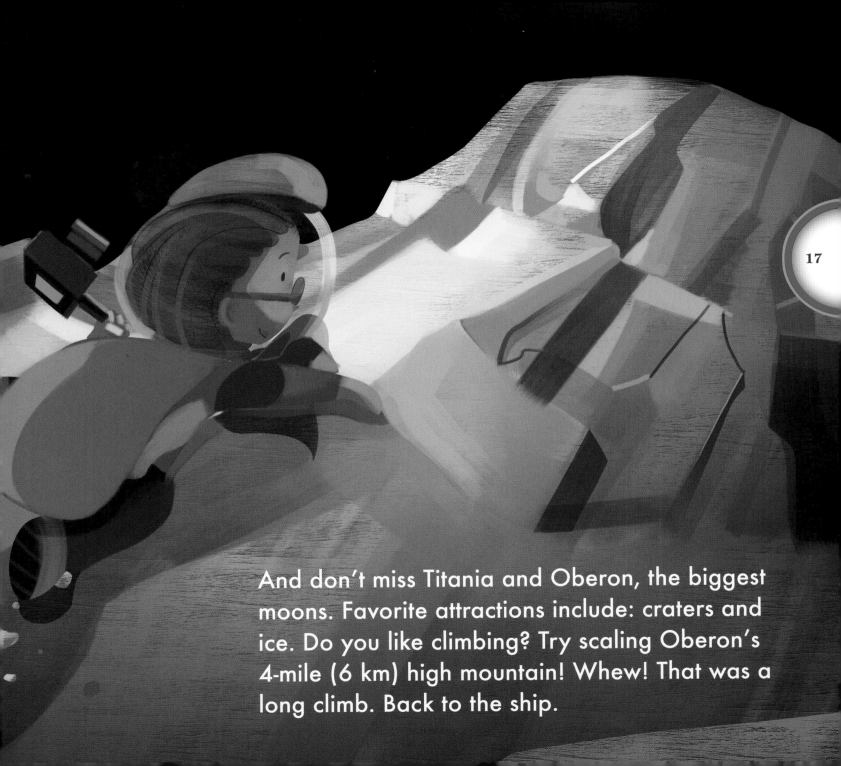

And don't miss Titania and Oberon, the biggest moons. Favorite attractions include: craters and ice. Do you like climbing? Try scaling Oberon's 4-mile (6 km) high mountain! Whew! That was a long climb. Back to the ship.

Hey, there are icicles in your eyes!
Oh. You must miss home.
Time to go.

18

LIMBRIEL

There.
That's better.
Home sweet
bedtime snack.

19

Uranus may be an exciting (and dangerous) place to visit, but you *really* wouldn't want to live there.

20

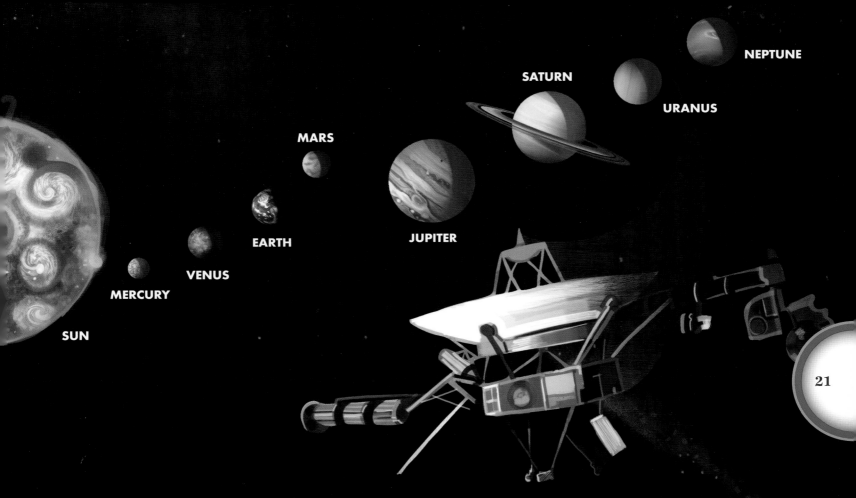

SUN

MERCURY

VENUS

EARTH

MARS

JUPITER

SATURN

URANUS

NEPTUNE

How Do We Know About Uranus?

We can't actually go to Uranus. A spaceship would run out of fuel before it got there. So how do we know about the planet? The unmanned space probe *Voyager 2* (1986) flew within 50,600 miles (81,500 kilometers) of Uranus. It took photos and gathered data. It radioed the information back to Earth.

Earth vs. Uranus

	Earth	Uranus
Position in solar system	Third from Sun	Seventh from Sun
Average distance from Sun	93 million miles (150 million km)	1,784 million miles (2,871 million km)
Year (time to orbit Sun)	365 days	84 Earth years
Day (sunrise to sunrise)	24 hours	17.24 Earth hours
Diameter	7,926 miles (12,756 km)	31,763 miles (51,118 km)
Mass	1	14.37 times Earth
Air	Oxygen and Nitrogen	Hydrogen, helium, and methane
Water	About 70% covered with water	Likely has water-ice in the clouds and slushy water in its interior.
Moons	1	27 known moons
Cheerios	Earth has Cheerios — yummy!	Umbriel has a ring that looks like a Cheerio, but it's a land feature, not food.

Glossary

atmosphere The mixture of gases that surrounds a planet.

gas The form of a substance in which it expands to fill a given area.

gas giant One of the four outer planets made up mostly of gases.

helium A light colorless gas that does not burn. It is often used to fill balloons.

hydrogen A colorless gas that is lighter than air and catches fire easily. It can also be used to fill balloons, but it's not recommended.

methane A colorless, odorless, flammable gas made of carbon and hydrogen.

moon A body that circles around a planet.

planet A large body that revolves around a sun.

pressure The weight of air or water pressing down on something.

rings Bands of dust or ice particles that revolve around a planet.

shepherd moon A moon that keeps one or more rings in place with its gravity.

Read More

Aguilar, David A. *11 Planets: A New View of Our Solar System.* Washington, D.C.: National Geographic, 2008.

Mist, Rosalind. *Uranus, Neptune, and the Dwarf Planets.* Mankato, Minn.: QEB Publishing, 2009.

Owens, L.L. *Uranus.* Mankato, Minn.: Child's World, 2011.

Sparrow, Giles. *The Outer Planets.* Mankato, Minn.: Smart Apple Media, 2012.

Websites

NASA Kids' Club
http://www.nasa.gov/audience/forkids/kidsclub/flash/
NASA Kids' Club features games, pictures, and information about astronauts and space travel.

StarChild: A Learning Center for Young Astronomers
http://starchild.gsfc.nasa.gov/docs/StarChild/
Click on Solar System to read facts about all the planets.

Voyager: The Interstellar Mission
http://voyager.jpl.nasa.gov/science/uranus.html
Learn about *Voyager* and *Voyager 2*'s discoveries about Uranus.

Welcome to the Planets: Uranus
http://pds.jpl.nasa.gov/planets/choices/uranus1.htm
View slideshows of the best photographs taken of Uranus, plus hear captions read aloud.

About the Author

Bridget Heos is the author of more than 40 books for children and teens, including *What to Expect When You're Expecting Larvae* (2011, Lerner). She lives in Kansas City with husband Justin, sons Johnny, Richie, and J.J., plus a dog, cat, and Guinea pig. You can visit her online at www.authorbridgetheos.com.

About the Illustrator

Daniele Fabbri was born in Ravenna, Italy, in 1978. He graduated from Istituto Europeo di Design in Milan, Italy, and started his career as a cartoon animator, storyboarder, and background designer for animated series. He has worked as a freelance illustrator since 2003, collaborating with international publishers and advertising agencies.